선교 유업 계승과
비서구권 선교운동

INHERITING THE MISSIONARY LEGACY AND
THE EMERGENCE *of*
MISSIONARY MOVEMENTS
in **NON-WESTERN REGIONS**

선교 유업 계승과 비서구권 선교운동

2025년 11월 7일 초판 1쇄 발행

지은이 조다윗

도서출판 비전출판사
주소 서울특별시 서대문구 가재울로2안길 33 (03693)
전화 02-6414-7864
이메일 visionpd2@hanmail.net
홈페이지 www.wmuv.net
등록번호 제 312-2013-000011호

ISBN 979-11-87120-22-3 (03230)

© 조다윗 2025

Inheriting the Missionary Legacy *and* the Emergence *of* Missionary Movements *in* Non-Western Regions

by David Cho

Copyright © 2025, by David Cho

이 책의 저작권은 저자와 도서출판 비전출판사가 소유합니다.
신저작권법에 의하여 한국 내에서 보호를 받는 저작물이므로
무단전재와 복제를 금합니다.

Research tasks *on* the Origins *of* the Remaining Arab Peoples
Copyright 2025. Missionary David Cho and Vision Publishing House all rights reserved.

선교 유업 계승과
비서구권 선교운동

조다윗 선교사 지음

INHERITING THE MISSIONARY LEGACY AND
THE EMERGENCE *of*
MISSIONARY MOVEMENTS
in NON-WESTERN REGIONS

David Cho

비전선교단
VISION

차례

머리말	9
감사의 말	12
선교 유업 계승과 비서구권 선교운동 발생 가능성	15

1 **서언** — 15

2 **연구 관점 및 사례(case) 적용 패러다임** — 19
   (1) 예수님과 열두 사도들 사역의 두 구조 — 21
   (2) 바울 선교 사역의 두 구조 — 24
   (3) 윌리엄 캐리의 근대 선교 추동 요인 — 27
   - 서구 보편교회 내 지상 명령 복원과 해외선교회,
     파라처지 구조 조직 주창
   (4) 랄프 윈터의 현대선교이론 정리 중 — 29
     <하나님의 구속적 선교의 두 구조> 이론

3 **비서구 선교운동 발생 가능성 사례별 현장 연구** — 31
   (1) 중국교회 - 핍박을 불구한 내륙 본토 기독 저력과 — 31
                  지도력들의 선교운동 의지
   (2) 몽골교회 - 기동력에 의거한 빠른 선교 비전의 수용 — 37
   (3) 남미교회 - 코미밤(COMIBAM) 중심의 사례 — 38
   (4) 인도교회 - 역동성과 정제 사이에서 — 41
   (5) 한국교회 - 선교운동 황혼기와 국제 선교지도력 — 43
                  계승 전환기의 기로에서

참고도서, 문헌 — 48

Contents

Preface — 55

Thanks to — 59

The Succession of Mission Heritage and the Possibility of Mission Movements Emerging in the Non-Western World — 61

1. **Introduction** — 61

2. **Research Perspective and Case-Application Paradigm Beyond the Limitations of Research** — 67
   (1) The Two Structures in the Ministry of Jesus and the Twelve Apostles — 69
   (2) The Two Structures in Paul's Missionary Ministry — 72
   (3) William Carey's Driving Factors in the Rise of Modern Missions — 76
      - Restoration of the Great Commission within the universal Western church and the advocacy of overseas mission societies as a para-church structure
   (4) Ralph Winter's Summary of Modern Mission Theory: The Two Structures of God's Redemptive Mission Theory — 78

3. **Case Studies in the Possibility of Mission Movements Emerging in the Non-Western World** — 81
   (1) The Chinese Church – The Christian Strength of Mainland China Despite Persecution, and Leaderships' Will for the Mission Movement — 81
   (2) The Mongolian Church – Readiness to Embrace a Rapid Mission Vision Rooted in Mobility — 88
   (3) The South American Church – The Case of COMIBAM — 91
   (4) The Indian Church – Between Dynamism and Refinement — 94
   (5) The Korean Church – At the Twilight of the Mission Movement and at the crossroads of the transition period of the succession of international missionary leadership — 97

Reference, Sources — 102

일러두기

이 글은 선교타임즈가 주최한
선교타임즈 2025 태국 포럼 및 태국 중부지회 선교사 수련회에서
발제되었고,
랄프윈터 박사가 창간한
국제전방개척선교저널(IJFM)의 자매지인
『전방개척선교(KJFM)』 26년 1, 2월호에 게재되었습니다.

머리말

10여 년 전 빌리그래함 전도협회 통해 발효된 call2all 세계선교전략회의를 섬기면서, 비서구권 선교 운동 추동에 세계선교지도력들의 각고의 노력과 섬김을 보며 함께 할 수 있었다. 국제 의장은 서구인이었으나, 인도에 선교사로 헌신해 선교운동을 추동시키는 자리매김에 있었고, 그는 담담하게 브론즈 헤어인 서구인보다 블랙 헤어의 비서구인이 더 많은 선교사 군대로 일어날 것에 대한 비전을 받았다고 했다.

이제 더욱 그러한 비전이 가까워져 가는 이때, 몇 가지 비서구권 선교운동 추동에 있어서 반복되지 않고 시행착오를 보완할, 소견을 머리말로 대신하고자 한다.

유럽 에든버러 선교대회가 대륙을 넘어선 복음과 선교의 선명성이 희미해져가며 WCC화 되어 자유주의 기독교마저 포용된 때에 여러 신학적 어젠다가 유럽에 존재해도, 다시 대륙을 넘어선 복음에 선명성을 지닌 미주 중심으로 시작된 로잔대회가 전도자 빌리그래함등을 통해 추동되어, 존 스토트 등 고명한 목회자의 비평적 지지와 랄프 윈터 같은 걸출한 현대선교전략 이론가를 통해 선교운동으로 구체화되고 복음주의적 기독교의 축이 유럽에서 미주로 전이되는 후광을 낳았다.

비서구권 선교운동은 이제 역동성을 갖출 터이나, 서구와의 일부 주도권 겨루기를 할 필요가 없겠다. 한국 리더들은 서구에 이어 비서구권 선교운동을 구체적으로 실행해 2만 8 천여 명까지 장기선교사를 보내본 경험이 있고 토착화된 사례와 모델링을 일군 흔적이 있으나, 윌리엄 캐리, 랄프 윈터 같이 명징한 세계선교운동 전략이나 선교이론을 스스로 도출해 기독교 세계를 정렬시켜 섬겨본 적이 있다고 보긴 어렵다.

다만 한인 선교사는 아시아인이면서 선교 운동 발생에 장기선교사를 보낸 실제 사례를 가진 구성원으로 역동성 가운데 실제와 정제가 긴요한 비서구권 전역에 촉매자나 코디네이터로서의 촉진자 역할을 감당할 수 있다. 또한 서구 이론의 합리성과는 대비되게 관계나 존재적으로 연합하는 비서구권 특성과 아시아의 중국, 인도, 몽골, 남미, 아랍 등에 특성을 이론과 조화시켜 비서구인이 하나 되어 선교하는 방식을 역시 추동 예비할 수 있겠다.

세상과 다르게 하나님 나라에서는 서로 간 섬김을 통해 지도력이 구체화된다. 지성 이론, 존재 관계, 감성 열정, 의지 등 각기 서로 다른 특장점을 가진 세계가 어우러져 선명하게 선교운동 추동을 위해 기독유업의 총체성을 서로 수혈하며 섬길 때 서구를 이어 비서구권에서도 본격적으로 대륙을 넘어서 장기 선교사를 보내는 흐름이 더욱, 곧 일어날 것이다.

2025년 10월 26일 주일

조다윗 선교사

감사의 말

책이 나오기까지 많은 영감에 자양분이 되어 준 믿음의 선진들과 더불어, 교정과 편집 작업을 도와준 유경은 간사, 임아란 간사 고상한 북디자인을 해 준 권혁기 간사, 김예은 간사 영문 번역을 맡아준 손은혜 간사, 박보아스 선교사 비전 선교 공동체와 함께하는 350여명의 선교 사역자들 모두 감사하다.

말씀과 함께 살기 위해 공동체의 삶을 마다않고 더불어 함께 하는 아내와 은빛, 시후, 안녕이를 비롯한 가족들은 내 보석들이다. 우리가 아니더라도 누군가를 통해 주님이 어두운 시대를 밝힐 말씀의 횃불을 드실 것이나 말씀이 우리와 함께 하심에, 그래서 감사하다.

INHERITING THE MISSIONARY LEGACY AND
THE EMERGENCE *of*
MISSIONARY MOVEMENTS
in **NON-WESTERN REGIONS**

선교 유업 계승과
**비서구권
선교운동**

선교 유업 계승과
비서구권 선교운동 발생 가능성[1]

조다윗 선교사[2]

1
서언

구약시대를 닫는 말라기서 마지막 말씀[3]은 사회과학적 측면으로 비춰 봐도 시대와 역사를 관통하는 통찰력이 담겨 있다. 즉 메시야의 길을 예비하기 위해 아버지의 마음을 자녀에게 돌이키고 자녀의 마음을 아비에게 돌이키겠다는 전조는 인류 역사의 한계와 문제의 핵심을 통찰력 있게 담고 있는 측면이 있다. 왜냐하면 인류 역사의 구분은 바로 이 문제로부터 비롯되기 때문이다. 인류 역사를 나누는 시대성

---

1 본 글은 선교타임즈에서 주최한 2025년 태국 해외포럼 중, '비서구 중심의 선교(Polycentric Mission)와 세계 선교의 미래' (강대흥 KWMA 사무총장)에 후속 발제로 발표되었다.

2 선교타임즈 세계문서선교협의회 법인이사장, 『선교타임즈』, 『전방개척선교』 공동발행인, 비전선교단 대표.

3 말4:6

구간의 표지는 사실 전대 인류의 정신성과 시대성에 대한 후대 시대 정신성의 반역이다. 곧 고대에 인류가 신봉해 왔던 미개한 종교 정신성을 중세가 일어나 체계적 종교 정신성(종교권력)으로 타도하고 근대가 일어나 사회적·이성적 합의의 정신성(사회권력, 정치권력)으로 중세까지 아비들이 신봉했던 종교정신성이 역사의 문제였음을 지적, 타도한다.[4]

또한 오늘날에 현대는 근대의 이성적·사회적 합의정신성(사회권력, 정치권력)에 대한 신뢰보다 축적의지의 정신성(경제권력)을 대체 우위로 역사를 주도하는 권력에 방향을 선회하고 있다. 즉 인류의 역사는 전(前)시대에 인류와 아비들이 이룩한 정신성에 대한 자녀 시대성으로 부터의 문제제기, 타도와 반역으로 얼룩져왔다.[5]

그러나 예수 그리스도를 통한 기독교 유업은 아담들끼리 반역하는 방식의 역사와는 근본적으로 궤적이 다르다. 반목했던 역사를 화평케 하고 하나님을 향한 순종을 적층

---

4 브리태니커 편찬위원회, 『근대의 탄생』, 이정인 옮김, 아고라, 2014.
5 조다윗, 『차세대 선교지도력과 집단트랙』, 비전선교단, 2021, 23p.

한다. 선지자와 율법으로 살아온 구약의 세례 요한을 통해 하나님 나라 일에 바통을 넘겨받아 예수가 완성한다. 아브라함과 이삭과 야곱의 하나님은 시대를 통해 기독교 유산을 전달하고 계승·확장할 전세대와 후세대를 연결하여 기독교 유업을 이루어 오셨다. 인생들을 통해 기독교 유업에 전통이 유전이 되는 오류도 있었지만 대국적으로는 연약한 인생을 택한 하나님의 역사는 지속된 세대 도킹과 세대 계승, 서구와 비서구 기독유업연대 등을 통해 유업이 전달되고 더욱 확장되어 갈 수 있다.

바야흐로 한국 교회에서 세계로 보낸 선교사들이 폭발적으로 증가하여 한반도 선교 운동이 이루어진지 30년에서 40년을 바라다보는 중요한 전환기다. 25년에서 40년이면 성경에서는 한 세대의 계수다. 한 세대가 지나 한국 선교사의 상당수가 은퇴나 은퇴기를 앞두고 있다.[6] 따라서 20-40대에 한반도 해외 선교 계승의 세대를 적극적으로 발굴하고 찾

---

[6] 장기 선교사의 연령 분포에서 50대 이상이 69.25%를 차지하고 있으며, 60대 이상의 선교사는 29.42%를 차지하고 있다. 반면, 30세 이하의 선교사 수는 6.51%이다. 전년과 대비하면 50대와 60대의 비율만 소폭 늘어나고, 기타 연령대는 모두 감소하였음을 알 수 있다.(한국선교연구원, 2024)

아 유업을 이어가지 않으면 운동의 특성상 축소와 위태가 있을 수 있다.

한편 1800여 년 동안 해외선교를 본격 감당했던 그룹은 서구였다. 이제 비서구권의 기독 인구가 세계 기독 인구의 절반에 육박하나 서구 기독 유업은 축소와 부침의 기로에 있기도 하다.[7] 그에 따라 기독 유업의 대륙을 넘어선 선교운동이 계속 추동되기 위해서는 서구를 이어 비서구권 선교운동 발생 가능성이 긴요한 시점이기도하다.

본고는 세대를 이은 선교 유업의 계승, 한반도 선교운동의 지속과 가능성을 간단히 요약, 진단해보고(이전 저술과 관련 포럼에서 상세히 3부작으로 다각적으로 다루었음으로 간략 진술), 비서구권 선교운동 가능성을 비서구권 국가 사례 연구(case study) 임상과 비선구권 선교운동의 한국교회 한인 선교 지도력의 역할에 대해 상세 진술하고자 한다.

---

[7] 한마디로, 기독교 교회는 교회 역사의 아주 초기 몇 해를 제외한 어느 시기보다 큰 지리적 재편을 지난 50년 동안 경험했다. "20세기 말의 전형적인 그리스도인은 더 이상 유럽 남성이 아니라 라틴아메리카나 아프리카의 여성이다." (데이너 로버트) 마크 A. 놀, 박세혁 역, 『복음주의와 세계 기독교의 형성』, IVP, 2015, p.28-31

2
연구 관점 및 사례(case) 적용 패러다임

비서구권 선교운동이 추동될 가능성을 찾는 노력이 기독유업에 이어지면서 서구 선교운동과 비서구 운동이 대립항이거나 그에 따라 보완을 넘어 단절 혹은 전면 수정의 관계성 속에서 비서구권 선교운동의 출현을 설명하려는 유혹이 있다. 근·현대 서구 선교운동의 일부 한계와 부작용을 인식하면서도 위와 같은 견해에 완전히 다 동의하기 어렵다.

유럽 대륙 바깥에 본격적인 서구 선교운동이 오대양 육대주 너머 선교해 온 측면이 있는바 근대 윌리엄 캐리(William Carrey)의 주창을 통해 서구 보편교회 내에 지상명령의 복원과 해외선교회 조직 등, 선교단체의 지상명령을 수행할 두 구조가 구축되었다. 또한 이러한 근·현대 사역의 두 구조를 성경적·선교학적으로 이론 정립, 정의한 랄프 윈터(Ralph D. Winter)의 모달리티(Modality)·소달리티(Sodality)의 두 구조로서의 선교운동 추동에 대해 강력한 틀을 제공하였다.

근·현대 서구 선교운동이 일부 폐해와 약점을 노출한 것도 사실이나, 길게는 로마 서구교회 출현 이후 1,800년, 짧게는 근·현대 200여 년 동안 꾸준히 해외로 장기선교사를 보낸 거의 유일하다시피 한 집단이었다. 그 운동력과 모델, 이론 제공에 있어서 검증된 선교운동의 거국적 발생이 거의 유일한 패러다임인 셈이다. 비서구권 선교운동이 이러한 서구 선교운동의 약점을 반면교사 삼고 이를 보완할 필요가 있겠으나, 비서구권 선교운동 추동은 현재 역동기에 막 진입한 맹아기일 뿐이며, 서구권에서 응용한 선교 이론과 전략·패러다임, 현장 등을 외면한 채로 서로를 검증할 수조차 없다. 이러한 지평 안에서 근·현대 선교 추동에 막대한 영향을 미친 윌리엄 캐리, 랄프 윈터 등은 서구인이어도, 초대교회 유업과 성서적 지평에서 선교운동의 발생 요인의 두 가지 구조, 이른바 소달리티, 모달리티의 복원과 협력을 통해 선교운동을 견인해 왔다는 점에서 그들이 주창하거나 추동시킨 선교패러다임이 온전히 서구적인 것만이라고 하기에는 무리가 있다. 엄밀히 말하자면 성경에 나타난 이 두 구조는 서구기독교가 발효되기 전의 것이기 때문이다. 따라서 이 소고는 랄프 윈터 등이 주창한 근·현대 선교 발생의 두 가지 구조에 입각하여 패러다임을 진술, 서구권 선교운동을 계승·보완해 일어날 비서구권 선교운동 발생 요소와 현장의 사례 연구에 기본 평가 패러다임 렌즈로 작동할 것임을 밝힌다.

(1) 예수님과 열두 사도들 사역의 두 구조

예수님이 초림 하셨을 때 그는 인간의 몸을 입고 오신 성자 하나님이셨기에 권능과 기적, 새롭고도 큰 가르침, 겸손하고 온유한 성품과 죄의 역사와 타협하지 않는 불굴의 거룩함에 의지 등등을 나타내시며 탁월하고도 흠잡을 데 없는 균형 잡힌 사역적 모델링의 정점을 보이셨다. 의아하게도 그분은 독자적으로 그 누구하고도 비견될 수 없는 자신의 탁월함과 비상함을 가지고 하나님 나라를 건설하실 수도 있었겠지만 그분이 처음 한 사역은 갈릴리의 형편없는 인생들을 찾아가셔서 하나님 나라의 일들을 함께할 자들을 모으시는 일이었다. 인간적인 관점에서 예수님의 도전은 무모해 보이는 일이었다. 그분이 감당할 수 없는 규모의 하나님 나라에 관한 일들을 말씀하셨기 때문이 아니라, 자신의 탁월함을 상식적 규모 이하로 추락시킬 인생 군상들에게 하나님 나라의 일들을 동참할 것을 호소하시고 실제로 그런 형편없는 인생들을 자신이 건설할 하나님 나라의 일들에 실제로 참여시키고자 이

끌고 다니셨다는데 있다. 명백히 그분의 행동과 기저의 의도 속에는 그들에게 비단 하나님 나라의 일들만 알려주려고만 부른 것이 아니라 하나님 나라의 건설에 참여케 하시려고, 그들이 참여했던 모든 세상일들을 정지시키고서야 그들이 예수님을 따를 수 있는 권리를 부여했다. 그냥 가르침을 받으라는 게 아니라 명백히 참여해야 할 일이 있다는 투였다. 따라서 예수님의 초림 사역 기저의 일차적 목표는 보내는 팀을 형성하는데 있어 보인다.[8]

신약을 잘 고찰해 보면 초림 때 예수님은 유대와 이방의 경계 갈릴리를 두루 오고 가시며 한 지역에 얽매이지 않으시고 이곳저곳에서 복음을 전파하실 뿐, 한 지역에 뿌리내릴 로컬 교회 이식에는 관심이 별로 없으신 듯했다. 오늘날의 지역 교회라고 말할 수 있는 한 지역을 정하시고 매주 설교하는 로컬교회를 개척하기보다 오히려 두루 다니시며 따를 제자와 사도들을 모으시고 이동하며 복음을 선포하는 모바일 선교

---

[8] 예수님은 내향적인 제자들의 관점을 외향적으로 바꾸도록 말씀하셨다. 예수님의 선교 동심원은 무한하다. 제자들이 복음을 들고 가야할 곳은 땅 끝까지이다.
폴 피어슨, 임윤택 역, 『선교학적 관점에서 본 기독교 선교운동사』, CLC(기독교문서선교회), 2009, p.55.

팀을 구축하시는데 주력하셨다. 이는 이른바 **보내는 선교팀, 소달리티 구조의 역점, 추동**인 셈이다.⁹

예수님은 초기 사역에서 하나님 나라 초기 사역의 모티브가 지역마다 수많은 사람들을 구심력 없이 느슨하게 묶어 신앙 공동체를 짓는 일보다 장차 하나님 나라의 구심력이 될 헌신된 제자군들이 예수님과의 밀도 있는 상호작용을 통해 사역을 감당할 수 있는 팀이 되기를 원하셨다. 곧 예수님 승천 후 하나님 나라를 위해 예수님처럼 사역할 수 있는 사역팀을 빌딩하시고 계속 이동하며 보내시고, 그 뒤에 그들을 통해 오늘날에 교회라 말 할 수 있는 지역마다 네트워크 될 수 있는 신앙 공동체가 받아내지는 시즌을 그리셨음에 틀림없다.

오순절 이후 예수님의 이러한 접근은 삼천 명, 오천 명에 걸친 대규모 회심 사건이 일어나면서 보다 전략적인 것으로 드러난다. 이것은 이른바 **보편로컬교회, 모달리티 구조의 본격 추동**인 셈이다.¹⁰

---

9   눅10:1~16
10 행2:41, 4:4

(2) 바울 선교 사역의 두 구조

안디옥교회의 지역교회 구조로부터 파송된 바울과 그 선교팀은 지역과 지역을 넘어 이동하고 팀을 이루어 복음을 전하며 파라처치 구조를 담은, 선교단체와 지역교회 두 구조의 협력 양상이다.[11]

바울은 한 지역에 교회개척에 접근하기에 앞서 성령의 인도하심에 기조를 따라 전략을 세울 뿐 일관된 기조를 가지고 사역한 패턴이 잘 보이지 않는 편이다. 성령의 지혜를 좇아 사역한다는 것은 모든 것을 아시는 주님 앞에 그 지역에 대한 성육신과 개척능력에 있어 탁월함을 보이는 것으로 증명되었다.

그러나 이러한 바울의 임의대로 부는 성령의 바람을 좇는 사역 속에서도 유난히 일관된 사역적 기조를 고찰할 수 있

---

[11] 사도행전 13장은 선교적인 사건이다. 이 사건을 통해 최초의 선교단체가 조직되었다. 선교단체를 통한 선교는 사도행전의 선교원리일 뿐 아니라 전 역사에 나타난 선교원리이기도 하다.
폴 피어슨, 위의 책, p.65.

는데 그것은 바울이 교회 개척을 위해 독자적 개척 접근을 한 것이 아니라, 항상 이동하는 팀을 리쿠르트하고 팀을 통해 미복음화 지역 내 교회 개척에 도전했다는 점이다.[12] 지역 교회 개척을 위해 전혀 개인적, 독자적 접근을 했던 아니라 모바일(mobile)하는 훈련된 교회구조를 만들어 협업적 교회 개척에 돌입했다.[13]

그의 전략은 생명력 있고 깊은 영감과 교훈을 준다. 바울의 선교팀은 지속적이고 연속적인 사역이 가능했다. 심지어 바울이 복음에 대한 지역적 저항과 거부 때문에 쫓겨나는 최악의 상황이 와도 팀 사역자들이 사역을 지속하거나 아니면 현지인조차 집단적 개척의 연속성에서 계속 복음을 증거하고 지역에 로컬교회 개척구조를 이어 가려했다. 왜냐하면 그들이 바울을 통해 본 신앙의 형태는 고립무원의 개인적 신앙만이 아니라 팀을 통한 공동체적 신앙에서 지역교회를 배태

---

[12] 빌4:2~4, 골4:7~11
[13] 선교단을 조직한 것은 교회확장에 가장 중요한 방법 중 하나였다. 바울과 바나바, 바나바와 마가, 베드로와 마가, 바울, 실라, 디모데, 그리고 누가 선교단은 초대교회 확장사에 중요한 역할을 했던 여러 선교단의 일부에 불과하다. 선교단은 최초의 선교조직체였다.
폴 피어슨, 위의 책, p.107.

했기 때문이다.

따라서 바울의 팀 사역은 적대적이고 핍박의 환경 속에서도 불굴의 자생력을 가지고 자라갔다. 바울의 팀 사역을 통해 음부의 권세를 이기는 교회의 천국 권세(네 고백 위에 내가 내 교회를 세우리니 음부의 권세가 이기지 못하리라, 마 16:18)는 개인 신앙이 아니라 교회를 통해 더욱 효과적으로 발휘된다는 것이 증명되었다.

바울의 팀 사역은 현지의 리더십 배양과 이양에서 탁월한 전이 속도를 보였다. 바울이 사역한 지역들은 길어야 2-3년, 핍박 때문에 짧게는 데살로니가 교회처럼 3주정도 밖에 가르치지 못하고도 현지에 자생적인 복음 전파의 흐름을 남겼다. 이러한 선교팀 사역은 바울만을 통해 복음이 독점적으로 전파되는 구도만은 아니었기에 바울이 핍박 때문에 불가피하게 현장을 이탈할 때도 이동하는 팀들, 그의 팀원들-디모데, 디도, 누가, 마가, 브리스길라, 아굴라 들을 통해 지속적으로 가르쳐졌다. 종종 바울 팀이 떠나고도 현지인 주도의 지역교회가 형성되어 그 지역에 자생적으로 복음이 전파되어졌다. 우리가 알고 있는 데살로니가교회, 갈라디아교회 등은 바울 선교팀이 개척해 지역교회로 남은 사례이다. 바울이 개척한 빌립보교회 등은 지역교회였으나 이동하며 대륙을 오고가며 복음을 전하는 바울 선교팀에게 연보를 보내기도 해 하나님 나라의 협력구조로 선순환 되었음도 우리가 주지하는 사실이다.[14]

(3) 윌리엄 캐리의 근대 선교 추동 요인
- 서구 보편교회 내 지상 명령 복원과 해외선교회, 파라처지 구조 조직 주창

윌리엄 캐리가 근대 선교의 아버지라고 불리는 까닭은 당시 유럽 보편교회 내에 팽배해 있던 지상명령에 대한 정지(停止)적 견해에 대해 성경적 복원을 주창, 논지적 설득의 준거를 마련했기 때문이다. 윌리엄 캐리는 당시에 서구 보편교회에 팽배했던 '지상명령이 사도 시대에 끝났다는 주장'과, 하이퍼 칼빈주의(Hyper-Calvinism)에 입각해 '이교도들이 개종할 때가 아직 도래하지 않았다는 주장' 등을 그의 논문 『이교도 선교방법론』 중 1부 <주님이 제자들에게 주신 선교 명령을 오

---
[14] 빌4:10~19

늘날에도 순종해야 하는가에 대한 연구>에서 성경의 텍스트와 맥락을 존중하여 논파해 지상명령을 현재 교회들이 순종해야할 대위임령으로 복원했다.[15]

이렇게 서구보편교회에 지상명령의 필요성을 각인하면서도 동시에 그는 지상명령 수행이 가능케 할 여러 현실적 동력을 주창, 제안 했는데 그 중에 하나가 파라처지 기능 즉 해외선교회와 선교위원회 조직을 통해 지속적으로 보내는 구조가 가능해야함을 역설한 일이다.

이러한 윌리엄캐리의 지상명령 복원과 해외선교회 조직 주창은 결국 잠자고 있던 유럽 서구교회를 깨워 유럽 밖으로 기독 유업이 나아가는 선교의 당위성을 제공했으며, SVM, 캠브리지7 선교운동이 추동되는데 이론적 배경이 되었으며 그들로 해외선교회를 조직케 하는 추동의 저변이 되어 결국

---

15 그러나 위에서 열거한 그 어떤 경우도 우리 기독교인들이 주님의 선교 명령을 순종하지 않은 데 대한 변명이 될 수 없다. 정결 예식에 관한 규정과는 달리 선교 명령은 취소된 적이 없으며, 또한 수행해야 할 명령의 대상이 없기 때문에 지킬 필요가 없다고 변명할 수도 없다.
변창욱, 「윌리엄 캐리 '이교도 선교 방법론'」, 장로회신학대학교 세계선교연구원, 2008, p.40.

근대 선교가 가능케 했다.

(4) 랄프 윈터의 현대선교이론 정리 중 〈하나님의 구속적 선교의 두 구조〉 이론

랄프 윈터는 로잔선교대회 등을 통해 세계 현대 선교 운동 이론에 결정적 영향을 미친 학자이다. 랄프 윈터는 〈하나님의 구속적 선교의 두 구조〉라는 글을 통해 모달리티, 소달리티 구조를 선교운동 추동에 핵심적 상보 구조로 명징하게 이론화했다.[16] 이는 성경적 상황 지평뿐만 아니라 선교 역사 속 선교운동의 추동 요인을, 카톨릭과 수도원 운동, 진젠도르프와 모라비안교도, 근대 대학 설립과 학생선교운동 발생 등 서구 선교운동의 추동을 이 두 구조의 이해를 통해 바라보게 했다. 또한 성경 텍스트 내에서도 이런 두 가지 구조가 발견된

---

[16] 모달리티는 성별이나 연령 구분 없이 누구나 그 구성원이 될 수 있는 하나의 조직 공동체다. 반면 소달리티는 연령, 성별, 혹은 결혼 유무에 따라 제한받는 조직 공동체. 따라서 소달리티 회원이 되려면 성인으로서 모달리티 회원이 되어야 할 뿐 아니라 또 한 번 헌신하는 제2의 결단을 해야만 한다. 이 두 용어를 이러한 개념으로 사용하면, 교단이나 지역 교회는 모달리티에 속하며, 선교회나 지역 교회 각종 남녀 선교회는 소달리티에 속한다.

랄프 윈터, 임윤택 역, 『랄프 윈터의 비서구 선교운동사』, 예수전도단, 2012, p.261.

다는 점에서, 초대교회, 중세, 근대, 현대 속 선교운동의 두 구조를 명징하게 살펴볼 수 있는 관점과 패러다임을 제공했다 볼 수 있다. 따라서 이러한 패러다임과 관점 응용 속에서 비서구권 선교운동의 추동 가능성도 고찰해보고자 한다.

3
비서구 선교운동 발생 가능성 사례별 현장 연구

(1) 중국교회 - 핍박을 불구한 내륙 본토 기독 저력과 지도력들의 선교운동 의지

중국교회 원로들은 1억 5천만의 성도들을 중국 각지에 핍박 상황 속에서도 일궈왔다. 그 핍박과 박해 가운데에서도 중국교회 원로들은 주님께 기도하고 매달리며 고난 가운데 은혜를 구해왔는데 기도하면 할수록 중국 내륙만이 아니라, 중국 서부 국경 밖 중앙아시아와 중동 등지로 선교사를 보내라는 촉구와 거룩한 부담을 느끼게 되었다.[17]

한국교회 원로들이 만인제사장 민족이 되어야 한다는 부담으로 2만 여명의 선교사를 해외로 내보냈던 것과 같이, 중국교회 원로와 리더들은 위와 같은 촉구에 반응해 중국 성

---

17 1976년 제 1회 중국 세계 복음화 대회가 홍콩에서 개최된 이래 선교 협력과 세계 선교 운동이 확산 되었다. '중국 교회의 선교 비전은 그 범위에 있어 항상 세계적이었다. 지금 중국 안팎에 살고 있는 그리스도인들이 함께 힘을 합쳐 선교사를 보내고, 중국과 예루살렘 사이의 마을, 도시와 나라, 그리고 여러 종족 집단 안에 새로운 그리스도인 공동체를 형성하려고 한다.' (에녹 완(Enoch Wan), 2008)

도의 십일조 100만 선교사를 보내겠다는 다짐도 올려드렸다. (근·현대 이르러 본격화된 서구 유럽대륙 너머의 선교 가운데 2000여 년 동안 역대 문화권 장기 선교사 수를 40만으로 추산하는 경우가 있는데 그에 따르면 중국교회 리더들의 서원은 비서구권 선교 추동 가능성에 있어 경이적인 일일 수 있다.)

중국교회는 중국대륙 내에 막대한 핍박 상황 속에서도 1억 5천만 성도를 일군 저력이 있다. 현실적인 측면이 강한 민족성을 지녀 대륙 내에서는 전도자가 핍박 가운데 각동 각처로 흩어져 자생하는 교회들을 개척해왔다. 다만 전도자 자립을 저변으로 한 이러한 개척 구조는 타문화권 선교에는 약점으로 작용하는 측면이 있다. 근·현대 선교가 다시 시작되게 한 윌리엄 캐리는 대륙을 넘어선 선교 지상명령과 파라처치 구조의 복원 필요성을 강조함을 통해[18], 대륙을 넘어 간 선교사들 주변, 보편교회와 파라처치 역량이 함께 투여되어 지속적으로 비자 갱신 전문성과 영적 자원 소프트웨어, 하드웨어 구조를 본국을 통해 선교사와 함께 보내는 구조가 가능하게 했다.[19] 그러나 중국교회는 자국 내 전도자들이 다른 지방에 복음 전파를 위해 보내져도 이에 대한 모교회의 지원이 거의 전무하다시피 했다. 따라서 전도자 스스로가 생계를 해결하면

---

18 만일 신실한 기독교인, 목회자, 몇몇 개인이 모여 선교회(society)를 만들고 선교계획안, 선교사 선발 규정, 선교비 모금 방법 등에 관한 여러 규칙을 만든다고 가정해 보자. 다음으로 이런 선교회 산하에 '위원회'를 임명해야 한다. 또한 선교 위원회 위원들은 선교 사업을 감당하는 선교사들의 목적에 면밀한 주의를 기울이지 않으면 안 된다. 그러므로 나는 '침례교' 내에 이러한 선교회와 위원회를 조직할 것을 제안하는 바이다. 내가 뜻하는 바는 이런 조직을 단지 기독교의 한 교파에만 제한하려는 것이 아니다. 나는 우리 주 예수 그리스도를 진실로 사랑하는 사람은 누구나 어떤 방식으로든 이 선교회에 참여하기를 진심으로 바란다.
변창욱, 위의 책, p.101-103.

19 가장 흥미로운 것은 소달리티 조직의 힘을 이용하는 데 실패한 개신교회는 윌리엄 캐리의 유명한 책(이교도 선교 방법론)에서 이교도 개종 수단의 모색을 제안할 때까지 거의 300년 동안 선교를 위한 아무 조직을 갖지 못했다는 사실이다. 여기에서 캐리가 언급하고 있는 핵심 단어인 '수단(means)'이라는 말은 구체적으로 소달리티 조직이 필요하다는 뜻이다. 캐리의 소논문이 인쇄, 보급되면서 '이교도 개종을 위해 이러한 종류의 '수단'을 강구하는 일이 봇물 터지듯 일어나기 시작했다. 그 이후 몇 년 사이에 이와 유사한 목적을 위해 많은 선교회가 생겨나기 시작했는데, 32년 사이에 12개 선교회가 조직되었다. 캐리의 이 소책자는 종교개혁의 엄청난 영적 에너지가 분출되도록 함으로써 아마도 기독교 역사상 성경을 제외하고 다른 어떤 책보다 세계 선교에 가장 혁혁한 공헌을 세운 책이 되었다!
랄프 윈터, 위의 책, p.273-275.

서 개척지에 성도들이 생겨 스스로 자립하기까지 개인적 역량에 의지하여 본국 내에 다른 지역 개척을 감당해왔다. 이들은 이런 전도자 파송과 선교사 파송을 같은 개념으로 생각해 왔다. 따라서 해외에 비자 유지를 위한 전문단체나 교단차원의 견인, 파송 후 매달 지급하는 파송 후원비, 지속적인 맨 파워의 확충 등 선교사를 보내기 위한 다각적 파송 구조는 거의 생소한 개념이었다. 선교사가 자국 내 전도자와 마찬가지로 스스로 직업을 가지던, 비자 유지가 어려워 단기로 본국으로 돌아오건, 한 번 보내면 단회적인 파송 개념으로 끝날 뿐 지속적인 지원이나 지원구조가 거의 없어왔다.[20]

본인이 섬겼던 빌리그래함 전도협회에서 추동시킨 콜투올(call2all) 세계선교전략회의에서는 미성서공회 대표, 위클리프 본부대표, CCC 국제 총재, 와이엠(YWAM) 국제 대표 등 서구 선교 유업 가운데 해외로 선교를 내보내는데 가장 유

---

[20] 그러나 진행되고 있는 선교조차도 적절한 관리가 되지 못하고 지속적인 재정 후원부족, 타문화 적응에 어려움을 겪는 등의 이유로 매우 짧은 기간에 중도 귀국하는 일들이 발생하고 있다. 세계선교를 위한 간절한 기도는 중국 교회들에게 전반적으로 파급되지 않았다. 교회에서의 선교교육이나 동원사역은 미미하며, 혹 이미 선교사를 파송한 선교기구나 교회가 있기도 하지만, 선교사 파송과 관리에 있어서 아직 조직적이거나 장기적이지 못한 문제가 있다.
김종구, 『중국교회의 타문화권 선교운동』, 목양. 2020. p.47.

의미한 사역 실제가 있는 단체 대표 및 서구 지도자 50인을 모아 중국의 대표적인 5개 교단, 온주 황청 등의 대표지도력에게 선교 동원, 훈련, 보편교회 교단 역할, 선교단체 전문성 등을 이식하는 모임을 클로징 미팅으로 가져본 적이 있다.[21] 이러한 동아시아에 선교운동 계승을 위한 노력의 시기가 중국 보안상의 문제로 2015년 어간 몇 년간 열리다가 닫혔는데, 그 이후로 100만 선교사 운동에 더욱 몰입한 중국지도자들이 해외로 선교사들을 보내기 위한 열망이 가중되었다. 이후 교단 선교부, 파라처치 구조를 배우는 등의 효과로 요르단 등지에 중국 선교사들이 파송되어 나오기 시작하더라는 현장 보고를 간헐적으로 듣게 되었으나 단기선교사가 아닌 장기 선교사 파송의 흐름은 아직도 본격적으로 진행되어가고 있다고 보긴 어려운 실정이다.

선교 운동이 해외에서 언어·문화에 대한 흡수성이 유연한 청년 운동이라면, 중국 역시 기존 농촌 지하교회, 도시교회, 삼자교회 할 것 없이 도시중심에 모바일 매체로 인한 시대정신성과 세대차이가 커져 자국 내 기독 유업을 젊은이들에

---

21 조다윗, 위의 책, 38p.

게 수혈시키는 것도 난관이 있어 선교운동 발생에 있어 큰 도전이다. 종교법 개정 등으로 핍박과 통제가 더욱 강화된 것 역시 중국교회 선교 운동 발생에 어떤 양상으로 작용할지 두고 보아야할 문제다. 로잔세계선교전략회의 역시 중국선교운동 발생에 중차대성을 인정하여 중국 지도력 200인을 로잔모임에 초청하여 선교운동 전이를 위해 애써보려 한 적이 있으나 중국 당국의 중국 지도력 통제로 무산된 경험이 존재한다.

또한 중국 지도력들이 국력으로는 G2에 올라선 긍지와, 중화사상 등으로 서구 지도력의 선교 이양을 받아들이기에는 다소 긴장이 존재할 수 있고, 서구의 마인드 중심의 개념화, 이론, 전략, 훈련 등을 직접적으로 수혈받기에는 한국보다 유리하다 보기 어렵다. 중국 사람들은 마인드(mind)보다 소위 하트(heart) 중심의 감성적, 관계적 코드에 반응·감응하는 편이다. 반면 한국 선교지도력은 서구 전략 이론을 비서구권 장기선교 운동으로 토착화해본 경험이 있으며[22], 아시아인

---

[22] 한국선교계의 선구자로 평가받는 조동진 박사는 1910년 에딘버러 100주년 기념대회인 2010년 동경 대회에 작고한 랄프 윈터 박사가 예정되었던 세션의 강사로 지목, 초빙되었다. 관련 언론 인터뷰에서 조동진 박사는 랄프 윈터 박사에 대해 "윈터박사와 생각의 차이가 있으나 근본적인 방향은 같다. 그는 나의 선교 동역자요 존경하는 스승이며 멘토가 되었던 분" 이라고 직접 언급하였다.(크리스찬투데이)

으로 관계적이면서도 머리만이 아니라 마음, 가슴으로도 선교동기화를 전할 수 있는 만큼 기존 한국 선교지도력이 서구와 중국 사이에서 선교 이양에 촉매제, 매개체 역할을 할 수 있다 보여진다.

(2) 몽골교회 - 기동력에 의거한 빠른 선교 비전의 수용

몽골은 남방계 농경 중심의 중국 민족과는 달리 북방계 유목기마민족의 성향을 가졌다. 다분히 정주하기 보다는 대륙활보와 이동에 능했던 경험과 역사성을 지닌 만큼, 대륙을 넘어 복음을 전하는 선교 비전이 제시되면 몽골 교회와 그 지도력들은 쉽게 잘 수용하는 편이다. 큰 부족장이 다른 군소 부족을 규합하거나 지도력에 책임감을 가지는 역사 특성상 몽골복음주의연맹도 몽골지도력들이 이미 발 빠르게 구축하였다. 한번은 몽골 교회 지도력들이 한국에 방문했을 때 과거 몽골이 페르시아와 남아시아에 진출했을 당시 남겨진 몽골로이드 계통의 하자라 종족을 소개하자, 그들은 즉각 언어·문화가 비슷한 하자라 종족을 선교 대상으로 삼겠다고 입양하며, 곧 단기팀을 자체적으로 보낸 적이 있었다.

다만 선교비전에 대한 즉각적이고 기동력 있는 헌신을 보여준 몽골교회지만, 보편교회, 파라처지, 개인 간 다각적 헌신을 지속적으로 보이기에는 몽골교회 규모가 너무 작다. 현재 개신교 교회가 몽골 내부 전체에 약 525여개로 집계되며, 개신교 인구는 약 4만 5천여 명에 불과하다.[23] 이는 곧 기동력이 강한 몽골인들이 장기 선교사로 지원해도, 지속적이며 본격적으로 지원해줄만한 몽골 개교회가 매우 적은 형편임을 의미한다. 또한 말씀 기반에 신앙이 치밀하지 못해 이단들이 교회를 점유하고자 회유하는데 취약하여, 얼마 전까지 국제 위클리프, 와이엠, 미성서공회 측은 몽골 교회에 성경 보급이 다각화, 전국화 되도록 힘써왔다. 말씀과 기도에 균형 잡힌 선교사들이 발효, 파송 되려면 몽골교회 차원에 성숙이 아직 긴요한 상황이다.[24]

(3) 남미교회 - 코미밤(COMIBAM) 중심의 사례

---

[23] 2021 몽골 선교지수(한인선교사지원재단 및 한국세계선교협의회, 한인세계선교사협회 제공)

[24] 우리는 양적 성장에만 자족할 것이 아니라, 몽골에 영구하고도 성경적인 건강한 교회를 어떻게 세우느냐가 중요한 과제이다.
전호진, 『아시아 기독교의 과거와 현재 그리고 미래』, 영문, 2008, p.276

남미교회 지도력들은 비교적 젊은 40-50대 지도력이다. 그들은 라틴 아메리카 전역에 개신교 인구수가 5천 5백만 명에 육박하게 될 정도로 한참 부흥할 때 주역이었으며, 국가를 부흥시켜본 경험이 있다.[25] 그들 중에 특히 선교이론가 루이스 부시(Luis Bush)에 영향을 받아 에스네(Ethne) 대회 등을 통해 선교 비전을 공유하여, 25개국에 선교협의회를 만든 지도력이 코미밤(COMIBAM)[26]이라는 선교대회를 통해 네트워크를 형성한 리더들이다.[27] 필자는 그들을 만나 선교지도력에 관해 대담하며 교류했던 경험이 있는데 그들은 이미 개교회 부흥[28], 선교단체 전략 이론 흡수, 훈련 및 단체 형성 등

---

25 폴 피어슨, 임윤택 역, 『선교학적 관점에서 본 기독교 선교운동사』, CLC(기독교문서선교회), 2009, p.615-618.

26 이베로-아메리칸 선교 협력체(COMIBAM)는 스페인, 포르투갈, 미국과 캐나다의 히스패닉계, 그리고 세계 여러 지역의 라틴계 디아스포라를 포함한 25개국의 국가 선교 협력체(CMN)를 대표하고 연합하는 선교 운동이다.

27 https://comibam.org/es/nuestra-historia/

28 허버트 케인, 신서균·이영주 역, 『세계 선교 역사』, CLC(기독교문서선교회), 1993, p.202.

에 선교 역동기를 경험하고 있었다.[29] 브라질이 19,000여명의 선교사를 보낸 실제도 있었다.[30] 다만 그들은 브라질을 비롯한 남미 전반에 경제적 추락과 유동성에 취약했으며 한국의 장기 선교사 파송처럼 교단, 개교회, 선교단체, 개인에 다각적 헌신 협력을 통한 파송이 아닌 개인이 주체가 되어 해외에 나간 사례 전부를 선교사 파송으로 본다며, 한국 선교의 처치, 파라처치, 개인의 삼중 디멘션의 파송을 매우 동경하고 있었다. 개인이 이주한 모든 경험을 선교라 할 수 없는데 개인이 스스로 해외로 나가 소명을 지키며 재정적 지원이나 멤버 케어 없이 헌신해야하는 개인 선교사의 양산이 주된 선교동력이

---

29 1970년대 이후 라틴아메리카 복음주의 교회들은 세계 복음주의 인구 중 35%를 차지할 만큼 급성장했다. 1987년 제 1차 COMIBAM 선교대회를 기폭제로 해외 선교 및 타문화권 선교에 대한 선교 운동이 태동했다.
이영민, 「한국교회가 라틴아메리카 선교를 올바르게 수행하기 위해 고려해야 할 선교 전략」, 『미션인사이트』, 주안대학원대학교, 2012, p.82-99.

30 1976년에 조직되어 약 250개 브라질 선교단체의 연합 기관인 브라질타문화선교협회(AMTB)의 조사에 따르면, 2017년까지 15,004명에 머물던 브라질 선교사는 2022년에 19,000명까지 늘어났다.

라는 점에서 그들은 고민을 토로했다.[31]

(4) 인도교회 - 역동성과 정제 사이에서

인도는 근래 많은 영혼의 추수와 더불어 미전도 종족이 가장 많이 분포하는 지역이기도 하다.[32] 단일교회로는 한국이 가장 큰 교회를 가지고 있다가, 남미에 가장 큰 교회가 생겼으나, 곧 인도의 부흥으로 인도에 가장 큰 교회가 생겼다는 보고가 있다. 라인하르트 본케(Reinhard Bonnke) 목사가 이끌던 아프리카, 아시아의 대중 집회 부흥과 같은 양상이 인도 도처에서 나타나고 있다. 인도와 중국을 합치면 세계 인구의 절반이 포진되어 있고, 기독 유업이 이곳에서 계속 부흥한다면, 기독 인구의 상당수가 비서구권으로 전이된 만큼 이곳에 양적 면에 있어서만큼은 쇠락한 유럽보다 기독교의 축이 될

---

31 남미의 교회 지도자들은 열방을 복되게 하는 남미교회의 잠재적 역량이 아직까지 충분히 발휘되지 못하고 있다고 생각한다. 7천만이 넘는 이베로 아메리카 복음주의자들 숫자는 점점 더 증가하고 있으며, 이들은 지금보다 더 많은 선교사들을 보낼 수 있을 것이다. 우리는 선교사 숫자를 늘리는 것뿐 아니라, 우리가 파송하는 선교사들의 훈련과 후원과 목회적 돌봄을 더 강화하기 위해 노력하고 있다.
(카를로스 스코트, 2008)

32 2023년 인도선교협회(IMA)는 243개 단체와 6만 명의 선교사를 대표하고 있다. https://operationworld.org/prayer-calendar/06-21/

가능성이 있다.

 이러한 가능성에도 인도교회는 몇 가지 취약한 지점을 보인다. 현실성과 이익 관계에 대해 능한 남아시아 인도인들은 속설에 '어디서든 살아남는 상인 중국인들을 벗겨 이윤을 취할 사람들이 인도인이다'라는 말이 있듯 기독교에도 은혜보다 거래, 비즈니스 마인드가 침투하여 일면에서는 상업화와 별 다를 바 없는 미성숙이 문화화되어 있다. 남아시아인의 고질적인 카스트 계급문화도 기독 역량의 분화를 가져온다.[33] 힌두교의 다신교 사상이 유일신 여호와를 섬기는 신 중 하나로 편입시키는 희석도 고질적인 문제가 되어왔다.

 이런 인도인들이 자국에 미전도종족을 입양하고 품게 하여 역동적 선교가 가능할 수 있을까? 지정학적으로는 미전도종족이 산개한 남아시아 접근성이 쉽고, 비근한 문화권 공간에 대한 이해도 클 수 있다. 하지만 중국 서부의 55개 종

---

[33] 개종자들은 주로 하층계급 출신들이다. 이러한 사실은 특히 60%의 크리스천이 종래의 불촉천민(Untouchables), 현재의 부속계급으로 알려진 계층 출신인 인도에서 특히 그러하다.
허버트 케인, 위의 책, p.168.

족 등을 한 족이 지배 예속화해 온 역사가 선교에 걸림돌이 되는 것처럼 인도는 선교의 잠재력과 접근성은 좋을 수 있으나, 남아시아를 주도해 왔던 인도인에게 인근 미전도종족이 쉽게 마음을 열 수 있을지 조심스러운 접근이 긴요해 보인다.[34] 인도에서 언어문화를 넘어선 장기 선교사가 출현하려면 정제와 역동성이 동시에 필요해 보이는 과제가 있다 하겠다.[35]

(5) 한국교회 - 선교운동 황혼기와 국제 선교지도력 계승 전환기의 기로에서

한국교회는 민족의 원로들의 혜안으로 제사장 민족이 되어야 한다는 서원 아래 서구에 이어 거의 독보적이게도 2

---

34 인도인 타문화 선교사들은 일부가 외국에 나가 활동하지만 대부분 인도 내에 있는 언어와 문화가 다른 사람들을 위해 사역하고 있다.
폴 피어슨, 위의 책, p.670.

35 인도의 거대한 다양성 때문에 인도 선교단체는 지금도 여전히 자국 내 문화 경계선을 넘는 선교사를 보내고 있다. 그러나 인도 교회는 이제 눈을 들어 바깥세상을 바라보기 시작했다. 인도교회는 자국의 경계를 넘어서 세계 복음화에 대한 관심을 높이고 있다.(K. 라젠드란, 2008)인도 선교단체들이 자국 내 선교를 넘어 해외 선교사를 파송한 역사는 비교적 짧은 편이다. 인도 내 가장 큰 선교단체인 인도선교협회 역시 2천 년대 초반까지는 5만여 명의 선교사들을 자국으로 파송했다. 해외 장기 선교사 파송이 진전되는 중이나 더욱 무르익기까지는 실제적 과정이 필요할 것으로 보인다.

만여 명의 장기 선교사를 해외로 40여 년 동안 파송해왔다. 1,800년 동안 대륙을 넘어 해외 선교에 나서 비서구권에 복음을 통해 영적 근간을 만들어왔던 서구선교는 장단점 속에서도 최근까지 비서구권 선교운동에 균형과 지속성을 가지고 발생한 사례가 한국 외에는 희소하다는 점에서 서구 선교의 독보성을 인정하지 않을 수 없다. 다만 서구 유럽에 기독교가 교파·교단 단체 운동을 지키기 어려울 만큼 위태가 꽤 커져있고, 미국도 PC 운동 등의 여파로 성경적 다음 세대 교육이 대도시에서 쉽지 않고 바이블 벨트 정도만 복음주의 모판이 그 영향력을 해외로 보낼 수 있을 만큼 선교운동에 위기와 부침이 있다.

따라서 비서구권에 기독인구가 크게 증가세에 있고, 이제 비서구권에서 선교운동이 본격화 되어야 한다는 목소리가 높아지는 가운데 한국은 기독유업의 총체성을 해외로 장기 선교사 파송들을 통해 지속적으로 균형 있는 구조- 보편교회, 선교전문단체, 개인의 삼중 디멘션으로 보내본 거의 유

일하다시피 한 비서구권 나라다.[36]

따라서 이러한 한국교회와 한인선교사, 지도력은 비서구권 선교 운동 발생에 촉매제 역할을 감당할 수 있다. 중국, 남미, 인도 등지에서 꿈틀거리고 있는 기독교의 역동성이 대륙을 넘어 해외로 보내는 선교유업의 실제적 사례와 균형과 성숙으로 추동, 발효되기 위해선 한인 선교 지도력이 한인만이 아니라 비서구권 기독유업에 선교 운동을 추동시키는 매개 지도력의 역할이 부여되고 있다. 또한 루이스 부시가 남미 지도자이나 영어에 유려했고 마이클 오 같은 한인이나 영어가 가능한 한인 선교사가 서구의 영어권 선교운동 플랫폼에 지도력을 함께 혹은 대리 견인해야할 필요성도 증대될 것이다.

다만 한국 선교운동이 40년 간 발효되어, 이제 1,2세대 현장 선교지도력들이 은퇴기거나 은퇴기에 가깝고, 중간 세대

---

[36] 한국 선교사가 이처럼 빠르게 늘어난 데에는 한국 교회 자체의 부흥과 성장이 한 가지 중요한 요인으로 작용한다. 또한 전국적인 중보기도 운동과 다양한 선교 사역을 감당하고 있는 선교단체들이 세계 복음화를 위한 초교파 협력을 증진시키기 위해 존재하고 있다. 한국인은 복음전파에 매우 열정적이며, 가족 중심적이다. 또한 교육 수준이 매우 높다. 한국 선교사들은 상대적으로 문화적 친밀감을 느끼는 중국인, 무슬림, 불교권 사람들에게 잘 받아들여지고 있다.(한철호, 2008)

의 현격한 부재, 언어문화에 대한 유연성이 있는 20-30대 선교사 출현이 희귀해진다는 측면에서 한국선교운동은 국제 지도력을 요청받는 반면, 해외선교 유업이 한인 다음 세대에게 전달, 계승 되는 측면이 미약해지고 있는 위태도 사실이다.

그럼에도 출생 인구의 빈약, 기독유업의 축소 위기의 한반도에서도, 여전히 기독 유업에 주효한 그룹은 초대교회처럼 다수의 대중 무리보다 십자가를 지는 제자들이다. 일찍이 방지일 목사, 조동진 박사등은 한반도 기독, 선교유업 위태의 시기 앞에 초대교회 유업과 제자들로 회복탄력성이 가능하다고 진단, 소망하였다. 따라서 통일한국의 비전을 통해 동질성 있는 인구의 역동성, 이주민 유학생 국내 대거 유입으로 인한 선교 운동의 한반도 내에 타문화권 전이, 청년들 중 소수라도 제자도를 지녀 선교유업에 동참할 세대 잉태, MK, PK 등 다음세대의 선교기독유업 세대 전승을 통한 가담 등을 염두에 둔다면 한반도에서 선교운동의 국제적 흐름과 비서구권 선교운동, 지도력이 발생할 가능성이 여전히 있다.

INHERITING THE MISSIONARY LEGACY AND
THE EMERGENCE *of*
MISSIONARY MOVEMENTS
in **NON-WESTERN REGIONS**

참고도서, 문헌

· 김종구, 『중국교회의 타문화권 선교운동』, 목양, 2020.
· 랄프 윈터, 「하나님의 구속적 선교의 두 구조」, 1973.
· 랄프 윈터 외 공저, 정옥배 외 역, 『퍼스펙티브스 1』, 예수전도단, 2009.
· 랄프 윈터 외 공저, 정옥배 외 역, 『퍼스펙티브스 2』, 예수전도단, 2009.
· 랄프 윈터, 임윤택 역, 『랄프 윈터의 비서구 선교운동사』, 예수전도단, 2012.
· 마크 A. 놀, 박세혁 역, 『복음주의와 세계 기독교의 형성』, IVP, 2015.
· 박영환, 『네트워크 선교역사』, 바울, 2012.
· 변창욱, 『윌리엄 캐리'이교도 선교 방법론'』, 장로회신학대학교 세계선교연구원, 2008.
· 변창욱, 윌리엄 캐리의 선교신학: 『이교도 선교방법론』(1792)과 『세람포어 선교협약문』(1805)을 중심으로, p.288-318, 2019.
· 브리태니커 편찬위원회, 『근대의 탄생』, 이정인 옮김, 아고라, 2014.
· 사무엘 H. 마펫, 김인수 역, 『아시아 기독교회사』, 장로회신학대학교 출판부, 1996.
· 이민교, 『미스터 미션 조동진』, 사도행전, 2018.
· 이영민, 「한국교회가 라틴아메리카 선교를 올바르게 수행하기 위해 고려해야 할 선교 전략」, 『미션인사이트』, 주안대학원대학교, 2012, p.82-99.

· 임윤택, 『랄프 윈터의 기독교 문명 운동사』, 예수전도단, 2013.

· 전호진, 『아시아 기독교의 과거와 현재 그리고 미래』, 영문, 2008.

· 조다윗, 『차세대 선교지도력과 집단트랙』, 비전선교단, 2021.

· 폴 피어슨, 임윤택 역, 『선교학적 관점에서 본 기독교 선교운동사』, CLC(기독교문서선교회), 2009.

· 허버트 케인, 신서균·이영주 역, 『세계 선교 역사』, CLC(기독교문서선교회), 1993.

· 한국선교연구원 https://krim.org/

· 류재광, https://www.christiantoday.co.kr/news/207538, 2010.

· 선교지수 연구개발, http://mindexw.net/

· 이베로-아메리칸 선교 협력체(COMIBAM), https://comibam.org/

· 오퍼레이션월드, https://operationworld.org/

차례

머리말	9
감사의 말	12
선교 유업 계승과 비서구권 선교운동 발생 가능성	15
1 서언	15
2 연구 관점 및 사례(case) 적용 패러다임	19
(1) 예수님과 열두 사도들 사역의 두 구조	21
(2) 바울 선교 사역의 두 구조	24
(3) 윌리엄 캐리의 근대 선교 추동 요인	27
- 서구 보편교회 내 지상 명령 복원과 해외선교회, 파라처지 구조 조직 주창	
(4) 랄프 윈터의 현대선교이론 정리 중 <하나님의 구속적 선교의 두 구조> 이론	29
3 비서구 선교운동 발생 가능성 사례별 현장 연구	31
(1) 중국교회 - 핍박을 불구한 내륙 본토 기독 저력과 지도력들의 선교운동 의지	31
(2) 몽골교회 - 기동력에 의거한 빠른 선교 비전의 수용	37
(3) 남미교회 - 코미밤(COMIBAM) 중심의 사례	38
(4) 인도교회 - 역동성과 정제 사이에서	41
(5) 한국교회 - 선교운동 황혼기와 국제 선교지도력 계승 전환기의 기로에서	43
참고도서, 문헌	48

Contents

Preface   55

Thanks to   59

The Succession of Mission Heritage and the Possibility of Mission Movements Emerging in the Non-Western World   61

1. **Introduction**   61

2. **Research Perspective and Case-Application Paradigm Beyond the Limitations of Research**   67

   (1) The Two Structures in the Ministry of Jesus and the Twelve Apostles   69

   (2) The Two Structures in Paul's Missionary Ministry   72

   (3) William Carey's Driving Factors in the Rise of Modern Missions   76
   - Restoration of the Great Commission within the universal Western church and the advocacy of overseas mission societies as a para-church structure

   (4) Ralph Winter's Summary of Modern Mission Theory: The Two Structures of God's Redemptive Mission Theory   78

3. **Case Studies in the Possibility of Mission Movements Emerging in the Non-Western World**   81

   (1) The Chinese Church – The Christian Strength of Mainland China Despite Persecution, and Leaderships' Will for the Mission Movement   81

   (2) The Mongolian Church – Readiness to Embrace a Rapid Mission Vision Rooted in Mobility   88

   (3) The South American Church – The Case of COMIBAM   91

   (4) The Indian Church – Between Dynamism and Refinement   94

   (5) The Korean Church – At the Twilight of the Mission Movement and at the crossroads of the transition period of the succession of international missionary leadership   97

Reference, Sources   102

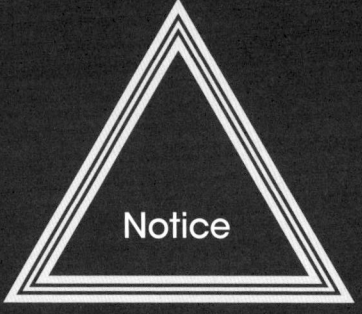

Notice

This paper was presented at
the Mission Times 2025 Thailand Forum and the Missionary
Retreat of the Central Thailand Chapter
hosted by Mission Times,
and was published in the January–February 2026 issue of
『Korean Journal of Frontier Missions (KJFM)』,
the sister journal of the International Journal of
Frontier Missions (IJFM) founded by Dr. Ralph D. Winter.

Preface

About ten years ago, while serving in the Call2All Global Mission Strategy Conference initiated through the Billy Graham Evangelistic Association, I had the privilege of witnessing firsthand the dedicated efforts and sacrificial service of global mission leaders striving to advance the non-Western mission movement. Though the international chairperson was a Westerner, he had long served as a missionary in India and had become as a driving force in the mission movement there. He calmly shared a vision he had received — that in the coming days, not the bronze-haired Westerners but the black-haired non-Westerners would rise as the greater missionary force.

Now, as that vision draws ever nearer to fulfillment, I would like to offer a few reflections in this foreword, hoping they may help the non-Western mission movement avoid repeated trials and refine its path forward.

When the Edinburgh Missionary Conference in Europe

lost its original evangelical clarity and shifted toward the WCC, embracing even liberal theology, new theological agendas emerged within Europe. Yet, in contrast, the Lausanne Movement—initiated from the Americas through evangelists such as Billy Graham—restored the clarity of the gospel that transcended continents. With the intellectual and pastoral support of leaders like John Stott and the strategic insights of missiologists such as Ralph Winter, it was concretized into a mission movement. Consequently, the center of evangelical Christianity transitioned from Europe to North America, leaving a significant historical imprint.

The non-Western mission movement is now poised to gain its own dynamism. However, there is no need for competition over leadership with the Western world. Korean mission leaders, following in the footsteps of the West, have already demonstrated what a non-Western mission movement can accomplish by sending approximately 28,000 long-term missionaries, developing contextualized mission models, and leaving tangible marks of indigenous ministry. Yet, it would be difficult to say that they have, like William Carey or Ralph Winter, produced distinctive global mission strategies or theories that have realigned and served the Christian world at large.

Nevertheless, Korean missionaries—being Asians who have themselves experienced sending long-term missionaries—are uniquely positioned to serve as catalysts or coordinators across the non-Western world, where both practical action and refinement are urgently needed. In contrast to the rational systemization of Western missiology, the non-Western world emphasizes relational and existential unity. By harmonizing these relational dynamics with the contextual characteristics of Asia—such as those found in China, India, Mongolia—as well as Latin America and the Arab world, non-Westerners may together pioneer a new collaborative paradigm of mission.

Unlike in the world, leadership in the Kingdom of God is formed through mutual service. As diverse worlds, each with their own gifts of intellect and reason, being and relationship, passion and will, come together in mutual exchange and service for the advancement of the mission movement, the fullness of the Christian legacy will be shared. Then, following the Western era, a new era will soon emerge—one in which the non-Western world sends long-term missionaries across continents with renewed vigor.

October 26, 2025, Sunday
Missionary David Cho

Thanks to

Thanks for all advanced of faith who was being inspiration of nourish- ment and also I thank you all staff Kyoungeun Yu, Hyeji Park, Aran Lim who helped proofreading and editing, and staff Hyeog-gi Gwon who did graceful design, and staff Siwon Park, Eunchong Park, Hee Myeong Kim who did translation, and about 350 mission staffs who works together in Vision Mission community.

My family a wife and Eunbit, Sihoo and Annyeong are my treasures who never reject the community lifestyle to live with the word of God. Of course the Lord will pick up the torch of His word to light dark age beside us, but that is why I am really appreciate His word is with us.

선교 유업 계승과
**비서구권
선교운동**

The Succession of Mission Heritage and the Possibility of Mission Movements Emerging in the Non-Western World[1]

Missionary David Cho[2]

1
Introduction

The closing words of Malachi[3], which conclude the Old Testament, contain insights that, even from a social-scientific perspective, pierce through the fabric of time and history. The prophetic sign that the hearts of fathers will be turned

---

1 This paper was presented as a follow-up to the lecture 'Polycentric Mission and the Future of World Mission' (Daehung Kang, Secretary General of KWMA) at the 2025 Thailand Overseas Forum hosted by Mission Times.

2 Chairman of Mission Times World Document Mission Council, 「Mission Times」, 「Korean Journal of Frontier Missions」 Co-Publisher, Vision Mission President.

3 Malachi 4:6

to their children and the hearts of children to their fathers in preparation for the Messiah's way, embodies the very limits and core problem of human history. This is because the divisions of human history stem from this issue. In fact, the markers that divide historical epochs can be understood as the rebellion of the spirit of one generation against the spirituality and worldview of the previous. Thus, the primitive religious spirituality that humanity clung to in antiquity was overthrown by the systematic religious spirituality (religious power) of the Middle Ages. The rational and social consensus of the modern era (social and political power) rose up to point out and overthrow the religious spirituality once revered by the fathers of the Middle Ages as the root of historical problems.[4]

Today, however, the modern trust in rational and social consensus (social and political power) is being replaced by the spirit of accumulation (economic power), which is

---

4 Encyclopaedia Britannica Editors, 『The Britannica Guide to the Ideas that Made the Modern World』, Encyclopaedia Britannica, Inc(2008).

increasingly steering the course of history. In other words, the history of humankind has been repeatedly marred by the next generation's challenge, overthrow, and rebellion against the spirituality their fathers had built.[5]

In contrast, the Christian inheritance through Jesus Christ follows a fundamentally different trajectory from this history of rebellion among Adams. Rather than perpetuating strife, it reconciles history and builds layer upon layer of obedience toward God. Through John the Baptist, who lived by the prophets and the Law, the baton of God's Kingdom work was passed on and brought to completion in Jesus. The God of Abraham, Isaac, and Jacob has, across the generations, linked forebears and descendants to deliver, pass on, and expand the Christian inheritance. Although human frailty has at times introduced distortions as traditions were passed down, God's overarching history has sustained this generational docking

---

5 David Cho, 「Next generation mission leadership and group track」, Vision Mission, 129p.

and succession, extending the Christian legacy through both Western and non-Western alliances.

Now, Korean missions stand at a pivotal transition. It has been about 30 to 40 years since the explosive rise of missionaries sent from Korea to the world. Biblically, 25 to 40 years constitutes a generation. After this generation, a significant portion of Korean missionaries now face retirement or are entering their retirement years.[6] Therefore, unless successors in their 20s to 40s are intentionally discovered and cultivated to carry forward the inheritance of Korean overseas missions, the movement may inevitably face contraction and vulnerabilityFor about 1,800 years, the group that primarily carried out overseas missions was the West. Now, although the Christian population in the non-Western world is approaching

---

[6] In the age distribution of long-term missionaries, those in their 50s and older account for 69.25%, while missionaries in their 60s and above make up 29.42%. In contrast, the number of missionaries under the age of 30 is 6.51%. Compared to the previous year, only the proportion of those in their 50s and 60s has slightly increased, while all other age groups have decreased.(KRIM, 2024)

half of the global Christian population, the Western Christian legacy stands at a crossroads of contraction and fluctuation.[7] Accordingly, for the missionary movement that transcends continents to continue, the emergence of a non-Western missionary movement to succeed the West has become a critical need.

This paper seeks to briefly summarize and assess the inheritance of the missionary legacy across generations and the sustainability and potential of the Korean missionary movement (noting that these matters have already been discussed in detail in three prior works and related forums, and will therefore be presented here in brief). Furthermore, it aims to examine the possibilities of non-Western missionary movements through clinical case studies of non-Western

---

[7] In short, during the past fifty years the Christian church has undergone greater geographic restructuring than at any other time in its history, except for the very earliest years. "The typical Christian at the end of the twentieth century is no longer a European male, but a woman from Latin America or Africa." (Dana Robert)
Mark A. Noll, Translated by Park Se Hyuk, 『The New Shape of World Christianity』, IVP, 2015, p.28-31

nations, and to present in detail the role of the Korean church and Korean missionary leadership within these non-Western missionary endeavors.

2
Research Perspective and Case-Application Paradigm

As efforts are made to identify the potential for non-Western missionary movements in succession to the Christian legacy, there is a recurring temptation to interpret them in opposition to Western missions—framing their emergence as rupture or total revision rather than complementarity. While it is necessary to recognize certain limitations and adverse effects of modern Western missions, it is difficult to fully endorse such a view.

Beyond the European continent, Western missionary movements expanded across the seas and continents. Through the advocacy of William Carey, the Great Commission was restored within the universal Western church, resulting in the organization of overseas mission societies. These societies established two structures through which the Great Commission could be carried out. Ralph D. Winter later provided a powerful framework for these by defining, on biblical and missiological grounds, the twofold structure of mission as modality and sodality. His articulation offered a strong paradigm for understanding the propulsion of modern missions.

Although modern Western missions exposed certain weaknesses and shortcomings, the fact remains that—whether broadly reckoned from the rise of the Roman Western church over 1,800 years ago, or more narrowly within the last 200 years of modern history—the Western church has been virtually the only body to consistently send out long-term missionaries on a global scale. Its movement, its models, and its theoretical contributions represent an almost unique paradigm of verified missionary expansion. While non-Western missionary movements may take Western shortcomings as lessons and seek to overcome them, they remain in their formative stage, only recently entering a dynamic phase. At this stage, they cannot yet be validated independently without reference to the theories, strategies, paradigms, and practices tested within the

Western context.

Within this perspective, figures such as William Carey and Ralph Winter—though Western—cannot be regarded as merely Western in their paradigms. From the standpoint of the early church heritage and the biblical horizon, their articulation of the two structures of mission, sodality and modality, represents not a Western invention but a recovery of patterns already present in Scripture, prior to the emergence of Western Christianity.

Therefore, this study will adopt Winter's paradigm of the two mission structures as a basic evaluative lens. It will use this paradigm to examine both the succession and supplementation of Western missions, as well as the emerging factors and case studies shaping the rise of non-Western missionary movements.

(1) The Two Structures in the Ministry of Jesus and the Twelve Apostles

When Jesus came at His first advent, He was the Son of God incarnate. He displayed power and miracles, profound and authoritative teaching, a character of humility and gentleness, and an uncompromising holiness that refused to yield to the power of sin. In this way, He revealed the pinnacle of a flawless, balanced model of ministry. Strikingly, although He could have built the Kingdom of God by Himself—through His unmatched excellence and divine authority—His very first act of ministry was to seek out the overlooked and marginalized lives of Galilee and gather them to share in the work of God's Kingdom. From a human perspective, this seemed a reckless decision—not because His vision for the Kingdom was too vast for Him to accomplish, but because He deliberately chose to entrust participation in the Kingdom to weak and ordinary people, whose inadequacy might appear to diminish His extraordinary excellence. Clearly, His intention was not merely to inform them about the work of the Kingdom, but to involve them in building it. To this end, He called them to leave behind their worldly occupations entirely, granting them the right to follow Him. His call was not simply "come and learn," but "come and participate." Thus, the primary goal underlying His first-advent ministry appears to have been the formation of a sending team.[8]

A careful reading of the New Testament shows that during His earthly ministry, Jesus traveled throughout Galilee—the boundary between Jew and Gentile—proclaiming the gospel widely rather than establishing a rooted local congregation in one place. Unlike the modern notion of planting a local church where He would preach weekly, His focus was to call disciples and apostles, to move with them, and to proclaim the gospel while forming a mobile missionary team. This reflects the essence and driving force of what is called the sending mission team, or the sodality structure.[9]

---

[8] Jesus instructed His introverted disciples to shift their perspective outward. The concentric circles of His mission are limitless, and the place where the disciples must carry the gospel is to the ends of the earth.
Paul Pierson, Translated by Im Yoon Taek, 『The Dynamics Of Christian Mission: History Through A Missiological Perspective』, Christian Literature Center, 2009, p.55.

[9] Luke 10:1~16

In His early ministry, Jesus did not primarily seek to loosely bind large crowds into regional faith communities without clear cohesion. Rather, His focus was to raise up a committed band of disciples who, through intensive interaction with Him, would be able to carry out the work of the Kingdom. After His ascension, this team would continue His mission—preaching, traveling, and being sent—until, through their ministry, networks of faith communities would emerge in various regions, becoming what we today recognize as local churches.

After Pentecost, Jesus' strategy became even more evident. Large-scale conversion events—such as the three thousand and five thousand who believed—revealed the strategic wisdom of His approach. This marked the beginning of the broader propulsion of the universal-local church, or the modality structure.[10]

(2) The Two Structures in Paul's Missionary Ministry

---

[10] Actd 2:41, 4:4

Paul and his missionary team, sent out from the local church in Antioch, traveled from region to region, forming mobile teams that proclaimed the gospel. Their ministry displayed a cooperative dynamic between the local church and a parachurch structure, embodying the dual structures of mission agencies and congregations working together.[11]

Although Paul, in approaching church planting, did not follow a rigid or uniform strategy—choosing instead to set his plans under the leading of the Holy Spirit—his ministry consistently demonstrated an incarnational and Spirit-empowered ability to adapt and establish new churches. Yet, even within this Spirit-led flexibility, one strikingly consistent pattern emerges: Paul never engaged in independent, solitary church planting. Rather, he always recruited and worked through a mobile missionary team, which collectively engaged unreached regions

---

11 Acts 13 is a missional event. Through this event, the first missionary organization was formed. Mission carried out through missionary organizations is not only a missionary principle of Acts but also a principle of mission evident throughout history.
Paul Pierson, the book in front, p.65.

in the challenge of church planting.[12] His approach was never an isolated individual effort but a collaborative mission that built mobile, trained church structures capable of cooperative church-planting.[13]

This strategy carried profound vitality, inspiration, and instruction. Paul's missionary teams ensured the continuity and sustainability of ministry. Even in the worst-case scenario—when Paul was expelled due to local resistance or persecution—the team members either continued the work themselves or facilitated local believers to carry forward the momentum of church planting. The model of faith they had witnessed in Paul was not that of an isolated, individual spirituality but of a community of faith that birthed local churches through team ministry.

---

[12] Philippians 4:2~4, Colossians 4:7~11

[13] Organizing missionary teams was one of the most important methods for church expansion. The missionary teams of Paul and Barnabas, Barnabas and Mark, Peter and Mark, Paul, Silas, Timothy, and Luke were only some of the many missionary teams that played a vital role in the expansion of the early church. Missionary teams were the first missionary organizations.
Paul Pierson, the book in front, p.107.

Consequently, Paul's team-based mission grew with resilient self-sustainability, even amid hostile and persecuting environments. His ministry demonstrates that the Kingdom authority of the church—"on this rock I will build my church, and the gates of Hades will not overcome it" (Matt. 16:18)—is expressed more effectively through the church as a community than through individual faith alone.

Furthermore, Paul's team ministry displayed remarkable speed in cultivating and transferring leadership to local believers. In regions where Paul ministered, his stay was often brief—sometimes two to three years, or in cases like Thessalonica, as short as three weeks. Yet even within such limited timeframes, his team left behind self-sustaining currents of gospel witness. This was possible because the spread of the gospel was not monopolized by Paul alone. When persecution forced him to depart, his team members—such as Timothy, Titus, Luke, Mark, Priscilla, and Aquila—continued teaching and building up the local believers. Frequently, even after Paul's departure, indigenous-led congregations emerged, carrying forward the mission autonomously. The Thessalonian church and the Galatian churches are well-known examples of congregations planted by Paul's missionary team. Churches such as the Philippians church, while being local congregations, also partnered with Paul's mobile missionary team by sending financial support as he crossed continents with the gospel. This mutual cooperation demonstrated a Kingdom-driven cycle of synergy between sending teams and local churches.[14]

(3) William Carey's Driving Factors in the Rise of Modern Missions
- Restoration of the Great Commission within the universal Western church and the advocacy of overseas mission societies as a para-church structure

William Carey is called the "Father of Modern Missions" because he challenged the prevailing suspensionist view of the Great Commission that had permeated the universal Western church of his time. By arguing for its biblical restoration, he

---

[14] Philippians 4:10~19

provided a persuasive theological foundation for missionary obedience. In his treatise An Enquiry into the Obligations of Christians to Use Means for the Conversion of the Heathens—specifically Part I, An Enquiry whether the Commission given by our Lord to His Disciples be still binding on us—Carey refuted, through careful attention to biblical texts and contexts, the claim that the Great Commission ended with the apostolic age. He also countered the assertions of Hyper-Calvinism, which held that "the time for the conversion of the heathen has not yet come." In so doing, he restored the Great Commission as the abiding mandate to which the contemporary church must remain obedient.[15]

While impressing upon the Western church the continuing obligation of the Great Commission, Carey simultaneously

---

[15] However, none of the cases mentioned above can serve as an excuse for us Christians not obeying the Lord's command to carry out His mission. Unlike the regulations concerning purification rites, the missionary mandate has never been revoked, nor can we excuse ourselves by claiming that there are no recipients of the command who require us to fulfill it. Byun Chang Uk, 『William Carey 'An Enquiry into the Obligations of Christians to Use Means for the Conversion of the Heathens'』, Presbyterian University and Theological Seminary Center for World Mission, 2008, p.40.

proposed the practical means by which it could be carried out. Chief among these was the establishment of a para-church structure: overseas missionary societies and missionary boards, which could provide a sustained and organized sending mechanism.

Carey's restoration of the Great Commission and his advocacy for the organization of mission societies ultimately awakened the dormant European church, providing the theological rationale for extending the Christian legacy beyond Europe. His vision laid the theoretical groundwork for later movements such as the Student Volunteer Movement (SVM) and the Cambridge Seven, which in turn organized overseas mission societies. Thus, Carey's initiatives served as a foundational impetus that made modern missions possible.

(4) Ralph Winter's Summary of Modern Mission Theory: The Two Structures of God's Redemptive Mission Theory

Ralph Winter, who exerted a decisive influence on the global modern mission movement through gatherings such as the Lausanne Congress on World Evangelization, articulated a crucial theoretical framework in his essay The Two Structures of God's Redemptive Mission. In this work, he defined the modality and sodality structures as complementary frameworks essential to the propulsion of mission movements.[16] This perspective not only illuminated biblical horizons but also explained the driving factors of mission throughout history. From Catholic and monastic movements, to Zinzendorf and the Moravians, and further to the founding of modern universities and the rise of student mission movements, the progress of

---

[16] Modality is an organizational community that anyone can join regardless of gender or age. In contrast, sodality is an organizational community that is restricted by factors such as age, gender, or marital status. Therefore, in order to become a member of a sodality, one must not only be an adult member of a modality but also make a second commitment of dedication. When these two terms are used in this sense, denominations or local churches fall under modality, while mission societies or various men's and women's missionary groups within local churches fall under sodality.
Ralph Winter, Translated by Lim Yoon Taek, 『The Twenty-Five Unbelievable Years, 1945-1969』, YWAM Publidhing, 2012, p.261.

Western mission can be understood through these two structures. Moreover, Winter demonstrated that these dual structures are discernible within the biblical text itself, providing a paradigm for examining mission movements across the early church, the medieval period, modernity, and contemporary contexts. Therefore, by applying this paradigm and perspective, one can also explore the potential drivers of mission movements within the non-Western world.

3
Case Studies in the Possibility of Mission Movements Emerging in the Non-Western World

(1) The Chinese Church
– The Christian Strength of Mainland China Despite Persecution, and Leaderships' Will for the Mission Movement

The senior leaders of the Chinese church have nurtured some 150 million believers across China, even under conditions of persecution. In the midst of suffering and hardship, these elders have continually sought the Lord in prayer, and the more they prayed, the more they sensed a divine call and holy burden—not only for China's inland regions but also for sending missionaries beyond China's western borders to Central

Asia and the Middle East.[17]

Just as senior leaders of the Korean church once felt the burden of becoming a "nation of priests" and responded by sending nearly 20,000 long-term missionaries overseas, so also leaders of the Chinese church have pledged to send one million missionaries—considered a tithe of their believers—in response to this sacred call. (Given that some estimates place the number of long-term missionaries over two millennia of Western missions at around 400,000, the Chinese leaders' vow can be seen as a remarkable indication of the potential for a non-Western-driven missionary movement.)

Despite severe persecution within the mainland, the

---

17 Since the first China World Evangelization Conference was held in Hong Kong in 1976, missionary cooperation and the world mission movement have expanded. 'The missionary vision of the Chinese church has always been global in scope. Now, Christians both inside and outside of China are joining forces to send missionaries and to establish new Christian communities in villages, cities, nations, and among various people groups between China and Jerusalem.'(Enoch Wan), 2008)

Chinese church has built up an extraordinary community of 150 million believers. With a pragmatic national character, evangelists under pressure have spread throughout the land, pioneering self-sustaining churches. Yet this grassroots model, dependent on the evangelist's own livelihood, has weaknesses when extended to cross-cultural missions. William Carey, who reignited modern missions, stressed the Great Commission as a mandate that transcends borders and emphasized the necessity of restoring para-church structures.[18] Through such structures, missionaries could be supported not only spiritually but also with practical resources—visa expertise, ongoing funding,

---

[18] Suppose that faithful Christians, pastors, and a few individuals come together to form a missionary society and establish various rules regarding mission plans, missionary selection criteria, and methods of raising mission funds. Next, such a society would need to appoint a "committee" under its authority. The members of this mission committee must also pay close attention to the purposes of the missionaries who undertake the work of missions. Therefore, I propose that such a missionary society and committee be organized within the Baptist denomination. By this I do not mean to limit such an organization to only one Christian denomination. Rather, I sincerely hope that anyone who truly loves our Lord Jesus Christ will, in some way, take part in this missionary society.
Byun Chang Uk, the book in front, p.101–103.

and organizational backing—provided by their home base. ¹⁹In contrast, in the Chinese Church, when evangelists within the country were sent to other provinces to spread the gospel, there was hardly any support from their home churches. Consequently, the evangelists had to rely on their own capacities to sustain themselves, taking responsibility for pioneering new areas within the country until a congregation was formed and became self-supporting. They regarded the sending of evangelists and the sending of missionaries as the same concept. Therefore,

---

19 What is most striking is that the Protestant church, having failed to harness the power of sodality structures, went nearly 300 years without any organization for mission—until William Carey, in his famous book An Enquiry into the Obligations of Christians to Use Means for the Conversion of the Heathens, proposed seeking ways to convert non-believers. The key word Carey highlights here, "means," specifically refers to the necessity of sodality organizations. As Carey's booklet was printed and circulated, efforts to devise such "means" for the conversion of non-believers began to spring up like a flood. In the years that followed, many missionary societies were founded for this very purpose—twelve within a span of just 32 years. By releasing the tremendous spiritual energy of the Reformation, Carey's little book perhaps contributed more to the advancement of world missions than any book in Christian history other than the Bible itself!
Ralph Winter, the book in front, p.273-275.

structures such as mission boards, denominational support systems, regular financial backing, and specialized manpower for sustaining long-term missionaries abroad have been largely unfamiliar. As a result, missionaries were expected to either support themselves with employment, return home when visas expired, or view sending as a one-time act without sustained support structures.[20]

While serving with the Billy Graham Evangelistic Association, I once witnessed such dynamics at a call2all World Missions Strategy gathering. Representatives of the most impactful Western mission organizations—the Bible Societies,

---

[20] However, even the mission work currently in progress often lacks proper management, resulting in missionaries returning home after a very short period due to ongoing financial shortages or difficulties in adapting to other cultures. The fervent prayer for world missions has not yet spread widely among Chinese churches. Mission education and mobilization within the churches remain minimal, and although there are some mission agencies or churches that have already sent missionaries, issues persist in that missionary sending and care are still neither systematic nor long-term.
Kim Jong Gu, 『Cross-Cultural Mission Movement of Chinese Church』, mokyangbook, 2020, p.47.

Wycliffe, CCC, and YWAM—along with 50 Western leaders, met with leaders from five representative Chinese denominations (including Wenzhou and Huangqing). The purpose was to introduce the Chinese church to the strategies of mobilization, training, denominational roles, and specialized mission agencies.[21] This effort to facilitate missionary succession in East Asia was pursued for several years until 2015, but eventually was shut down due to Chinese security issues. Yet in the wake of this closure, Chinese leaders became all the more committed to the vision of sending one million missionaries. Subsequent reports indicated that Chinese missionaries began to be sent, for example, to Jordan—especially as they learned from denominational mission boards and para-church models. However, the consistent flow of long-term missionaries has not yet fully taken shape.

If missionary movements are often driven by the flexibility and cultural adaptability of young people, China faces an ad-

---

21 David Cho, the book in front, 146p.

ditional challenge: passing on its spiritual legacy to younger generations. Rural house churches, urban churches, and the Three-Self Church alike are marked by generational divides heightened by mobile media and urban culture, making it difficult to transmit faith to the youth. Further, revisions to religious regulations have intensified persecution and control, raising questions about how these pressures will affect China's missionary movement. The Lausanne World Mission Strategy Conference once invited 200 Chinese leaders to a gathering, recognizing the immense importance of China's missionary potential. Yet governmental restrictions prevented their participation, showing how political factors continue to constrain such efforts.

In addition, among Chinese leadership, there may be a certain tension in accepting the transfer of missionary leadership from the West, due to their pride in China's rise to a G2 power and the influence of Sinocentrism. The Western mode of theory-driven, conceptual, and strategic approaches may not resonate as effectively with Chinese leaders, who are more relational and heart-centered in their responses. By contrast, Korean missionary leadership—having already contextualized Western mission strategies into a long-term, non-Western missionary movement—may serve as a bridge.[22] As fellow Asians, Koreans can communicate not only with the mind but also with the heart, enabling them to act as a catalyst and mediator between the West and China in this vital process of missionary succession.

(2) The Mongolian Church
– Readiness to Embrace a Rapid Mission Vision Rooted in Mobility

Unlike the agrarian and sedentary character of the southern

---

[22] Dr. Cho Dong-Jin, recognized as a pioneer of Korean missions, was invited as the speaker for the session originally scheduled for the late Dr. Ralph Winter at the 2010 Tokyo Conference, which commemorated the centennial of the 1910 Edinburgh Conference. In a related media interview, Dr. Cho stated regarding Dr. Winter: "Although there were differences in our thinking, our fundamental direction was the same. He was my fellow worker in mission, a respected teacher, and a mentor to me."(Christian Today)

Chinese peoples, Mongolia has historically been shaped by the nomadic equestrian culture of the northern steppe. With a heritage of mobility and continental expansion rather than settled stability, the Mongolian church and its leaders tend to readily embrace missionary visions that call for carrying the gospel beyond their own borders. Reflecting their history—where great chieftains united smaller tribes under a sense of responsibility and leadership—the Mongolian Evangelical Alliance was also quickly established by Mongolian leaders themselves. On one occasion, when Mongolian church leaders visited Korea and were introduced to the Hazara people, a Mongoloid group in Persia and South Asia descended from the Mongol expansion, they immediately "adopted" the Hazaras as a mission target, recognizing cultural and linguistic similarities, and soon after dispatched their own short-term team.

Yet while the Mongolian church has demonstrated impressive immediacy and mobility in responding to missionary visions, its small size limits its capacity for sustained, multi-dimensional commitment at the level of local churches, para-church organizations, and individuals. At present, there are only about 525 Protestant churches across Mongolia, with a Protestant population of roughly 45,000.[23] This means that even if Mongolian believers, known for their mobility, volunteer as long-term missionaries, there are very few Mongolian congregations capable of providing the sustained support necessary for such missions. Moreover, because the church's biblical grounding remains relatively weak, it has at times been vulnerable to the influence of sects seeking to co-opt congregations. For this reason, organizations such as Wycliffe, YWAM, and the Bible Societies have worked in recent years to diversify and expand Bible distribution throughout the country. At this stage, the maturity of the Mongolian church—particularly in developing missionaries deeply rooted in Scripture and prayer—remains a pressing

---

[23] 2021 Mongolia Mission Index (Provided by the Korean World Missionary Care Foundation, the Korean World Missions Association, and the Korean World Mission Council)

need for ensuring a stable and balanced mission movement.[24]

(3) The South American Church – The Case of COMIBAM

The leadership of the South American church is relatively young, mostly in their 40s and 50s. These leaders were central figures during a time when Protestantism expanded to nearly 55 million adherents across Latin America, and they had first-hand experience in leading national revivals.[25] Many of them, particularly influenced by mission strategist Luis Bush, shared a missionary vision through gatherings such as the Ethne Conference. Out of this, leaders from 25 countries established missionary councils and formed a continental network through

---

[24] We must not be content with mere numerical growth; the crucial task is how to establish a permanent, biblical, and healthy church in Mongolia.
Jeon Ho Jin, 『The Past, Present, and Future of Asian Christianity』, Young Moon, 2008, p.276

[25] https://comibam.org/es/nuestra-historia/

the COMIBAM[26] mission congress.[27] In my own encounters and dialogues with these leaders about missionary leadership, I found that they had already experienced revival in local congregations,[28] absorbed strategic theories from mission organizations, and developed training programs and mission structures.[29] In fact, there was a case where Brazil alone had sent

---

[26] The Ibero-American Missionary Cooperation (COMIBAM) is a missionary movement that represents and unites 25 national missionary cooperation bodies (CMNs) from Spain, Portugal, Hispanic communities in the United States and Canada, as well as Latin diaspora communities across various regions of the world.

[27] https://comibam.org/es/nuestra-historia/

[28] Herbert J. Kane, Translated by Shin Seo Kyun · Lee Young Joo, 『A Concise History of the Christian World Mission』, CLC(Christian Literature Center), 1993, p.202.

[29] Since the 1970s, Evangelical churches in Latin America have grown rapidly, coming to comprise 35% of the global Evangelical population. Sparked by the first COMIBAM Mission Congress in 1987, a missionary movement toward overseas and cross-cultural missions began to emerge.
Lee Young Min, 「Mission Strategies for the Korean Church to Consider in Order to Carry Out Missions in Latin America Effectively」, 『Mission Insight』, Juan International University, 2012, p.82-99.

approximately 19,000 missionaries.[30] Nevertheless, they faced vulnerabilities. Both Brazil and South America more broadly have been marked by economic decline and instability. Unlike Korea, where long-term missionary sending has been sustained through a multi-dimensional partnership of denominations, local congregations, mission agencies, and individuals, South American missions are often understood primarily as individuals going abroad. They tended to regard every case of personal migration as missionary sending. Many expressed deep admiration for Korea's "triple dimension" of sending—through church, para-church, and individuals working together. At the same time, they admitted their concern that not every migration can rightly be considered mission. The proliferation of self-supporting missionaries, who often pursue their calling without financial support or member care, has become the primary driving force of missions in South America, raising significant

---

30 According to a study by the Brazilian Association of Cross–Cultural Missions (AMTB), an umbrella organization founded in 1976 that unites about 250 Brazilian mission agencies, the number of Brazilian missionaries increased from 15,004 in 2017 to 19,000 in 2022.

challenges.[31]

(4) The Indian Church
– Between Dynamism and Refinement

In recent years, India has experienced a remarkable harvest of souls and at the same time remains the region with the largest concentration of unreached peoples.[32] Whereas Korea once had the world's largest congregations, later surpassed by South America, reports now suggest that the largest church may have emerged in India through its ongoing revival. Mass revival movements, similar to those led by Reinhard Bonnke

---

[31] Church leaders in South America believe that the potential of the South American church to be a blessing to the nations has not yet been fully realized. The number of Evangelicals in Ibero-America, now exceeding 70 million, continues to grow, and they could send out even more missionaries than they currently do. We are striving not only to increase the number of missionaries sent, but also to strengthen the training, support, and pastoral care of those we send. (Carlos Scott, 2008)

[32] In 2023, the India Mission Association (IMA) represented 243 organizations and 60,000 missionaries.
(https://operationworld.org/prayer-calendar/06-21/)

in Africa and Asia, are appearing throughout India. Considering that India and China together account for half of the world's population, if revival continues to spread in these regions, the center of Christianity could shift decisively to the non-Western world, surpassing Europe not only in numbers but also in global influence.

Despite such potential, the Indian church faces several weaknesses. South Asians are known for their pragmatism and transactional approach to life. A common saying goes, "If the Chinese are merchants who can survive anywhere, the Indians are those who will strip even the merchants for profit." Such tendencies have seeped into the church, where transactional attitudes and a business mindset often overshadow grace, producing a kind of immaturity that resembles commercialization. The entrenched caste system further fragments Christian capacity and unity.[33] In addition, Hindu polytheism has posed a chronic issue, as it tends to absorb worship of Yahweh into a pantheon of many gods, rather than preserving the uniqueness of the one true God.

Can Indians, then, effectively adopt and nurture unreached peoples within their own country for dynamic mission? Geographically, India is well-positioned, with many unreached groups scattered across South Asia, and culturally it possesses significant affinity with them. Yet, much like the Han dominance over 55 minority groups in western China has impeded mission, India's long history of cultural dominance raises the question of whether neighboring unreached peoples will easily open their hearts to Indian missionaries.[34] For India to produce

---

[33] Most converts come from the lower castes. This is especially true in India, where about 60% of Christians come from the groups formerly known as the Untouchables, now referred to as the Scheduled Castes.
Herbert J. Kane, the book in front, p.168.

[34] Some Indian cross-cultural missionaries serve abroad, but the majority are ministering to people within India who speak different languages and belong to different cultures.
Paul Pierson, the book in front, p.670.

long-term, cross-cultural missionaries capable of transcending linguistic and cultural barriers, both refinement and dynamism will be required in equal measure.[35]

(5) The Korean Church
   – At the Twilight of the Mission Movement and at the crossroads of the transition period of the succession of international missionary leadership

The Korean church, under the insight of the nation's elders who vowed that Korea should become a priestly nation, has sent

---

[35] Because of India's immense diversity, Indian mission agencies are still sending missionaries across cultural boundaries within their own country. However, the Indian church has now begun to lift its eyes to the outside world. It is increasingly turning its attention beyond its own borders toward world evangelization.(K. Rajendran, 2008) The history of Indian mission agencies sending missionaries overseas, beyond domestic missions, is relatively short. Even as late as the early 2000s, the India Mission Association, the country's largest mission organization, was sending about 50,000 missionaries within India itself. While progress is being made in sending long-term missionaries abroad, further practical steps will still be needed before this can fully mature.

nearly 20,000 long-term missionaries overseas for more than forty years, second only to the West. Western missions, which for 1,800 years ventured beyond continents to establish spiritual foundations in non-Western regions through the gospel, were unique in sustaining cross-continental outreach. Despite both strengths and weaknesses, Western missions remained the primary example of balanced and continuous cross-continental mission endeavors. In contrast, few non-Western countries besides Korea have sent long-term missionaries on such a scale. However, Christianity in Western Europe is now so fragile that denominational and church-based movements struggle to survive. The United States, too, faces challenges: the aftermath of PC(Political Correctness) movements makes biblical education for the next generation difficult in major cities, with only the Bible Belt maintaining enough evangelical strength to continue sending influence overseas. The overall Western mission movement faces crisis and decline.

Meanwhile, with the Christian population in non-Western regions rapidly increasing, calls are rising for mission movements to be rooted in these areas. Korea stands out as one of the few, if not the only, non-Western nations to have consistently sent long-term missionaries with a balanced structure across three dimensions: the local church, mission agencies, and individuals.[36]

Accordingly, the Korean church, Korean missionaries, and their leadership can serve as catalysts for sparking new mission movements in the non-Western world. As Christian dynamism stirs in China, Latin America, and India, the Korean church's legacy of cross-continental missions—grounded in balance, maturity, and concrete practice—positions it to play a mediating role in propelling these regions forward. Just as Latin American leader Luis Bush, fluent in English, influenced

---

[36] One important factor behind the rapid increase in Korean missionaries is the revival and growth of the Korean church itself. In addition, nationwide intercessory prayer movements and various mission organizations are engaged in missionary work, existing to foster interdenominational cooperation for world evangelization. Koreans are deeply passionate about evangelism and strongly family-oriented. They are also highly educated. Korean missionaries are generally well received by Chinese, Muslims, and Buddhists, with whom they tend to feel a relative sense of cultural affinity. (Han Chul-Ho, 2008)

mission thought globally, so too must Korean leaders—such as Michael Oh and other English-proficient Korean missionaries—step into Western mission platforms, either alongside or on behalf of Western leadership, to sustain global collaboration.

Yet, the Korean mission movement, having matured over forty years, now faces the retirement or near-retirement of its first and second generation of field leaders. The middle generation is notably sparse, and the rise of flexible, linguistically and culturally adaptable missionaries in their twenties and thirties has become rare. Thus, while Korean missions are increasingly called to international leadership, the transmission of mission legacy to the next Korean generation remains fragile.

Even so, despite declining birth rates and shrinking Christian influence on the Korean peninsula, the true sustaining group of faith has always been, as in the early church, not the large crowds but the disciples willing to bear the cross. Early leaders such as Pastor Bang Ji-Il and Dr. Cho Dong-Jin diagnosed the fragility of Korea's Christian and mission legacy but also expressed hope that resilience was possible through the model of the early church and committed disciples. Looking forward, if the vision of a unified Korea fosters dynamic energy within a homogenous population, if the influx of migrants and international students into Korea sparks cross-cultural mission within its borders, and if even a small number of youth embrace discipleship and mission legacy—whether through MKs, PKs, or next-generation believers—then the Korean peninsula may yet see the birth of a new generation carrying forward its mission heritage. This, in turn, could contribute meaningfully to the international flow of mission and the emergence of non-Western leadership in global missions.

References, Sources

- Kim Jong Gu, 『Cross-Cultural Mission Movement of Chinese Church』, mokyangbook, 2020.
- Ralph Winter, 「Two Structures of God's Redemptive Mission」, 1974.
- Ralph Winter, Steven C. Hawthorne, 『Perspectives on the World Christian Movement: A Reader』, William Carey Publishing, 2009.
- Ralph Winter, 『The Twenty-Five Unbelievable Years, 1945-1969』, William Carey Publishing, 2005.
- Mark A. Noll, 『The New Shape of World Christianity』, IVP Academic, 2013.
- Park Young Hwan, 『Network to View the History of Missions』, Paul Publishing, 2012.
- Byun Chang Uk, 『William Carey 'An Enquiry into the Obligations of Christians to Use Means for the Conversion of the Heathens'』, Presbyterian University and Theological Seminary Center for World Mission, 2008.
- Byun Chang Uk, Mission Theology of William Carey: Focused on William Carey's "An Inquiry"(1792) and "Serampore Covenant"(1805), p.288-318, 2019.
- Encyclopaedia Britannica Editors, 『The Britannica Guide to the Ideas that Made the Modern World』, Encyclopaedia Britannica, Inc, 2008.
- Samuel Hugh Moffett, 『A History of Christianity in Asia』, Orbis Books, 1998.
- Lee Min Kyo, 『Mr. Mission David Cho』, Actsbook, 2018.

- Lee Young Min, 「Mission Strategies for the Korean Church to Consider in Order to Carry Out Missions in Latin America Effectively」, 『Mission Insight』, Juan International University, 2012, p.82-99.
- Lim Yoon Taek, 『Ralph Winter's History of the Christian Civilization Movement』, YWAM Publidhing, 2013.
- Jeon Ho Jin, 『The Past, Present, and Future of Asian Christianity』, Young Moon, 2008.
- David Cho, 『Next generation mission leadership and group track』, Vision Mission, 2021.
- Paul Pierson, 『The Dynamics Of Christian Mission: History Through A Missiological Perspective』, William Carey International University Press, 2009.
- Herbert J. Kane, 『A Concise History of the Christian World Mission』, Baker Academic, 1978.
- Korea Research Institute for Mission https://krim.org/
- Ryoo Jae Gwang, https://www.christiantoday.co.kr/news/207538, 2010.
- Mission Index Research & Development, http://mindexw.net/
- Ibero-American Missionary Cooperation(COMIBAM), https://comibam.org/
- Operationworld, https://operationworld.org/